The American Republic

The Principles of Our Nation's Foundation

By: Tony Zore

The American Republic

Foreword

We are taught in school that we are an ideological nation. Where other nations form around a common bond of race or geography, Americans hold a common ideology. For this reason anyone can come to America and become an American. If this is true it follows that there is a bare minimum of ideology required to be an American.

What is that bare minimum? What is that ideology? These questions become increasingly important as Americans become increasingly divided. The answer may be the key to unifying us or the reason why we are forever divided. Like all fans of history, I looked back to try and find the answer to these questions. This book is the product of that search. I don't know whether it will help unify or divide us, but it is the best answer I can give. I tried to throw away all different conclusions people could reach from that bare minimum ideology while maintaining its core. I believe we have gotten away from many of these principles and so I expect any reader to have some disagreement, but I don't believe we can truly unify as Americans unless we can come back to that bare minimum of ideology that created our nation in the first place.

The American Republic

Chapter 1: Life, Liberty, and Property

> Rights are natural, they are universal, and they are a fundamental necessity to valid government.

Modern society has misconstrued the word 'right,' so badly that it no longer retains its meaning. Anyone claims the word for anything they desire and thus there is no meaning that it is anything but an entitlement you want. The American philosophy has a very specific meaning for the word. A 'right' is the ability to act without being oppressed. A right is not something given to you; it is a fact of your natural existence. Your right to Life is synonymous with the fact that you are alive. You, as a living person, have a right to Liberty because you take your own actions as a fact of nature. As a natural fact you will act to sustain yourself, give yourself shelter, and protect yourself. Property, in context of rights, is a means of accomplishing this because the same physical space cannot be both a farm field and a house at the same time. You cannot choose to use a log to make a chair if your neighbor is choosing to burn that same piece of wood. Property is a fact of interaction with this world. To make Property public does nothing to remove that ability to act, but delegates it to someone or a body of people who will make that choice for everyone else. To recognize private Property is to recognize an individual's right to determine what is to be done with the property, and thus a method of allowing people to live freely without having to ask the public for permission to act. In order to sustain your life and liberty, you must have the ability to own private property to use towards those pursuits. A right, or the ability to act without being oppressed, applies to everyone equally. To violate another person's property, freedom, or life is to oppress them and invites the same against you.

When Thomas Jefferson wrote the Declaration of Independence, he didn't bother to explain the definition of rights because he and all Americans saw it as a self-evident fact of nature's design.[*] The Declaration he wrote went on to explain that Governments are created among people to protect these natural rights and that governments are only valid by the consent of the people they are governing for this purpose. These concepts were not revelations being declared for the first

---

[*] "WE hold these truths to be self-evident, that all Men are created equal, that they are endowed by their Creator with certain unalienable Rights, that among these are Life, Liberty, and the Pursuit of Happiness" – The Declaration of Independence, 1776

time, but often stated beliefs that most Americans already held. Jefferson even faced accusations of plagiarism with the Declaration of Independence.[*1] The core body of Thomas Jefferson's cited explanation of rights and governments in the Declaration of Independence was essentially a simplified version of John Locke's, "Second Treatise of Civil Government." Locke argued that government can only derive just power from the consent of the governed and that people had individual rights to Life, Liberty, and Property as a fact of nature. When government became abusive of those rights, and all forms of appeal within the government had failed, Locke said it was the obligation of the People themselves to, "Appeal to Heaven," through armed combat. This concept was so influential in American philosophy that General Washington's ships sailed under a flag featuring a Pine Tree and the slogan, "Appeal to Heaven," taken directly from Locke's work.[2] The Massachusetts Navy also adopted the design for use on their ships.[3] Samuel Adams argued this same understanding of rights and government in, "The Rights

---

[*] "Richard Henry Lee charged it as copied from Locke's Treatise in government. Otis' pamphlet I never saw, and whether I had gathered my ideas from reading or reflection I do not know. I know only that I turned to neither book nor pamphlet while writing it. I did not consider it as any part of my charge to invent new ideas altogether, and to offer no sentiment which had ever been expressed before." – Thomas Jefferson to James Madison, 1822

of the Colonists." George Mason made the case in, "The Virginia Declaration of Rights." It was a universal understanding held and argued by the Founding Fathers.

The sentiment of natural rights as a requirement to valid government wasn't just held by all the Founding Fathers. It transcends generations in American history and is a necessary thread to America's social fabric. James Otis Jr. was an influential politician in the colonies prior to the American Revolution. He argued the concept before the Superior Court in Boston in 1761.[4] The argument Otis made was against the current acts of Parliament at the time, but he cited it as an existential struggle of all of English history.[*] John Adams stated this specific speech bore the American Revolution.[5] James Otis also foreshadowed the American Civil War when he argued these natural rights

---

[*] "These principles and these rights were wrought into the English Constitution as fundamental laws. And under this head he went back to the old Saxon laws, and to Magna Charta, and the fifty confirmations of it in Parliament, and the executions ordained against the violators of it, and the national vengeance which had been taken on them from time to time, down to the Jameses and Charleses, and to the Petition of Right and the [British] Bill of Rights and the [English] Revolution. He asserted that the security of these rights to life, liberty, and property had been the object of all those struggles against arbitrary power, temporal and spiritual, civil and political, military and ecclesiastical, in every age." – An Account of James Otis's speech, 1761

belong to everyone, black or white, in his work, "The Rights of the British Colonies Asserted and Proved."[*6]

Even before the Declaration of Independence, Thomas Jefferson argued for the abolition of slavery based off of natural rights. In 1770, he attempted to win freedom for the slave Samuel Howell in Howell vs. Netherland. His defense cited natural rights as a basis against the practice of slavery and a reason for the plaintiff to be set free.[†7] In the original copy of the Declaration of Independence, Jefferson even cited the legality of slavery as a tyrannical offense committed by

---

[*] "The colonists are by the law of nature freeborn, as indeed all men are, white or black. No better reasons can be given for enslaving those of any color than such as Baron Montesquieu has humorously given as the foundation of that cruel slavery exercised over the poor Ethiopians, which threatens one day to reduce both Europe and America to the ignorance and barbarity of the darkest ages." – James Otis, 1764

[†] "Under the law of nature, all men are born free, every one comes into the world with a right to his own person, which includes the liberty of moving and using it at his own will. This is what is called personal liberty, because [it's] necessary for his own sustenance. The reducing [of] the mother to servitude was a violation of the law of nature: surely then the same law cannot prescribe a continuance of the violation to her issue, and that without end, for if it extends to any, it must to every degree of descendants." – Thomas Jefferson, 1770

King George III.[*][8] The paragraph was removed in order to gain southern support for passage in the Continental Congress.

After the revolution, natural rights remained a permanent part of the American identity and a contradiction with the practice of slavery and the denial of women's suffrage. As the States of America became increasingly divided approaching the Civil War, figures such as Lincoln[9] and Frederick Douglas[10] cited the same natural rights found in the Declaration of Independence

---

[*] "He has waged cruel war against human nature itself, violating its most sacred rights of life and liberty in the persons of a distant people who never offended him, captivating and carrying them into slavery in another hemisphere, or to incur miserable death in their transportation thither. This piratical warfare, the opprobrium of infidel powers, is the warfare of the Christian King of Great Britain. Determined to keep open a market where men should be bought and sold, he has prostituted his negative for suppressing every legislative attempt to prohibit or to restrain this execrable commerce. And that this assemblage of horrors might want no fact of distinguished die, he is now exciting those very people to rise in arms among us, and to purchase that liberty of which he has deprived them, by murdering the people on whom he also obtruded them: thus paying off former crimes committed against the liberties of one people with crimes which he urges them to commit against the lives of another." – Draft of the Declaration of Independence, 1776

as the case for the abolition of slavery.* When slavery was finally abolished following the war, the Fourteenth Amendment continued this tradition of natural rights by affirming, "[no State shall] deprive any person of life, liberty, or property, without due process of law[.]" When it came time for women's suffrage, they also turned to the natural rights recognized by our Founders. In the

---

* "Our Declaration of Independence says: We hold these truths to be self evident: that all men are created equal; that they are endowed by their Creator with certain inalienable rights; that among these are life, liberty and the pursuit of happiness. That to secure these rights, governments are instituted among men, DERIVING THEIR JUST POWERS FROM THE CONSENT OF THE GOVERNED. I have quoted so much at this time merely to show that according to our ancient faith, the just powers of governments are derived from the consent of the governed. Now the relation of masters and slaves is, PRO TANTO, a total violation of this principle." – Abraham Lincoln, 1854

"Your fathers have said that man's right to liberty is self-evident. There is no need of argument to make it clear. The voices of nature, of conscience, of reason, and of revelation, proclaim it as the right of all rights, the foundation of all trust, and of all responsibility. Man was born with it. It was his before he comprehended it. The *deed* conveying it to him is written in the center of his soul, and is recorded in Heaven. The sun in the sky is not more palpable to the sight than man's right to liberty is to the moral vision. To decide against this right in the person of Dred Scott, or the humblest and most whip-scarred bondman in the land, is to decide against God. It is an open rebellion against God's government." – Frederick Douglas, 1857

1848 Declaration of Sentiments, Elizabeth Cady Staton cited the same body of natural rights in an amended form of the Declaration of Independence.[11]

Contemporaries redefine rights to mean anything they want. As a matter of course, this means the government will violate the natural rights of Americans to give entitlements to others. By creating a system where every individual could live freely without being oppressed in their actions, the American Republic established a system that recognized and protected our natural freedom. Being human, the implementation of this system has never been and will never be perfect. The standards of this system, however, have had the effect of creating emphasis on every individual's cause. Every person in American history has had the ability to point back to this standard of 'rights' when theirs are violated and has been able to say, "I, as an individual, am free as a fact of nature and you are wrong for oppressing me." In the American Republic, rights are natural, they are universal, and they are a necessity to valid government.

The American Republic

Chapter 2: Taxation and Representation

> All valid government requires consent of the governed.

"Government," is a monopoly of force sufficient to establish a set of social standards in a given geographic area. These standards can include everything from rules regarding property, practice of trade, speech, religion, or more. Kings proclaimed themselves to be the living Will of their country and thus, justified in setting these standards. English tradition had developed Parliament as a voice of the people and produced the belief that the King's powers came from their consent. Leviathan, by Thomas Hobbes, argued that consent was derived from the governed to establish the King who then was the living will. It was written as a response to the English Civil War of the 1640s and Hobbes himself served as a tutor for King Charles II.[12] Hobbes saw the Monarchy as a necessary 'Common Will' for the people.[*13] [14] His argument was that because people are naturally divided, absolute sovereignty must be placed in one person to give stability to a commonwealth. That

---

[*] See end notes.

monarch would be picked by the consent of the governed to protect themselves and would remain in power thereafter because to break that social contract would be to invite anarchy and chaos back into the country.[*]

If the Founders had followed Hobbesian philosophy, they wouldn't have rebelled. Instead they drew from John Locke's, "The Second Treatise of Government." Locke agreed that Consent of the Governed was a necessary precursor to validate the government but unlike Hobbes, he rejected such a thing as a 'common will' and saw that consent as being a

---

[*] "And for the other instance of attaining sovereignty by rebellion; it is manifest that, though the event follow, yet because it cannot reasonably be expected, but rather the contrary, and because by gaining it so, others are taught to gain the same in like manner, the attempt thereof is against reason. Justice therefore, that is to say, keeping of covenant, is a rule of reason by which we are forbidden to do anything destructive to our life, and consequently a law of nature. There be some that proceed further and will not have the law of nature to be those rules which conduce to the preservation of man's life on earth, but to the attaining of an eternal felicity after death; to which they think the breach of covenant may conduce, and consequently be just and reasonable; such are they that think it a work of merit to kill, or depose, or rebel against the sovereign power constituted over them by their own consent. But because there is no natural knowledge of man's estate after death, much less of the reward that is then to be given to breach of faith, but only a belief grounded upon other men's saying that they know it supernaturally or that they know those that knew them that knew others that knew it supernaturally, breach of faith cannot be called a precept of reason or nature." ~ Thomas Hobbes, Leviathan

continual necessity. He placed sovereignty in the individual People of a nation instead of its government.[*][15] His view was that valid government must derive its power and justification from the consent of the individuals who live in that area at all times. This view directly ties in to the belief of our natural freedom. Each of us having an individual will as a fact means that any claim to a 'common will' is either a majority consensus of individuals using force to impose themselves on others or one individual using force to impose their will upon others. It is a statement of fact that this can only happen if we allow it to through our consent.

James Otis Jr. cited Locke directly in many of his works including, "The Rights of the British Colonies Asserted and Proved,"[16] which outlined the case of

---

[*] "THOUGH in a constituted commonwealth, standing upon its own basis, and acting according to its own nature, that is, acting for the preservation of the community, there can be but one supreme power, which is the legislative, to which all the rest are and must be subordinate, yet the legislative being only a fiduciary power to act for certain ends, there remains still in the people a supreme power to remove or alter the legislative, when they find the legislative act contrary to the trust reposed in them: for all power given with trust for the attaining an end, being limited by that end, whenever that end is manifestly neglected, or opposed, the trust must necessarily be forfeited, and the power devolve into the hands of those that gave it, who may place it anew where they shall think best for their safety and security." ~ John Locke, Second Treatise of Government

taxation requiring consent of the governed as a matter of British Rights continuing from the Magna Carta to the time of the publication in 1764. James Otis's speeches and writings continually advocated taxation's link to representation throughout the 1760s and they repeatedly cite the longstanding practice of this as an British right.

Clause 14 of the Magna Carta required the King to summon the General Council of the Kingdom before levying taxes.[17] The General Council, at that time, consisted of powerful men throughout the Kingdom and the practice of calling a Council to levy taxes actually predated the Magna Carta as a tradition.[18] This tradition continued and was even a primary reason for the English Civil War of the 1640s.[19][20] It was again a cited right within the British Bill of Rights of 1689. [*21] Over and over again throughout English history, consent of the governed was a cited necessity before taxation. Thomas Jefferson and the Continental Congress echoed this right in the Declaration of Independence when they cited, "imposing taxes on us without our consent," as one of the offenses of the King.[22]

---

[*] "That levying money for or to the use of the Crown by pretence of prerogative, without grant of Parliament, for longer time, or in other manner than the same is or shall be granted, is illegal;" ~ British Bill of Rights 1689

When the Founders set up the Constitution, it was the House and not the Senate or the President that was given the power to tax and raise revenue. This was because the House of Representatives directly represented the People, unlike the Senate which was a body of Ambassadors from the States. National taxes were required to be proportionately applied to the States based off the amount of Representatives they had.[*] To the Founders it was as important that representation be linked to taxation as it was taxation being linked to representation. It was a two-way relationship.[†23] [24] [25] States were able to decide on their own standards for voting. Most required that someone be a property owner

---

[*] "Representatives and direct Taxes shall be apportioned among the several States which may be included within this Union, according to their respective Numbers," ~ US Constitution, Article 1 Section 2 (Prior to the 16th Amendment in 1913)
"All Bills for raising Revenue shall originate in the House of Representatives; but the Senate may propose or concur with Amendments as on other Bills." ~ United States Constitution, Article 1 Section 7

[†] "[I]f the jurisdiction of the national government in the article of revenue should be restricted to particular objects, it would naturally occasion an undue proportion of the public burdens to fall upon those objects. Two evils would spring from this source: the oppression of particular branches of industry; and an unequal distribution of the taxes, as well among the several States as among the citizens of the same State." ~ Alexander Hamilton, Federalist Paper 35

Additional quote from James Madison in endnotes.

and this was because most States taxed Americans by land and property, which was not difficult to acquire in a land full of wilderness.[26] [27]

The understanding that all valid government comes from the consent of the governed is synonymous with the concept of natural rights and so is taxation's relation to representation. All people are equal and band together in government for the protection of their equal rights. This is not a justification of the government to take any action, oppress the minority of any vote, oppress minority demographics, or to charge others for what we want in government. It means that the people, as individuals, are consenting to a common defense of their rights and share a common responsibility to that defense. The governing body is not synonymous with the 'will,' of the people it governs. Government is not entitled to take any action or dole out any cost of operation to the people without their consent. This is especially true if the actions or cost come at the deliberate expense of some people for the deliberate favor of others. In the American Republic, all valid government requires the consent of the governed.

The American Republic

Chapter 3: Freedom of Expression

> Rights exist as restraints against government
> specifically for when they're seen as detrimental.

People are naturally free. We create government because in that natural state people will infringe on each other's freedom. This tendency does not disappear with government and government's enforcement is, at best, a necessary evil encroaching on that natural freedom.[*28] Consent of the governed helps to minimize this encroachment by government. The rights we recognize tell the government that encroachment on these forms of our natural freedom is intolerable and that such encroachment violates the government's reason to exist. This applies specifically because those who run the government will see a need to curtail our freedom for what they believe to be the benefit of society. Few rights demonstrate this principle of 'rights as boundaries

---

[*] "Society in every state is a blessing, but government even in its best state is but a necessary evil; in its worst state an intolerable one; for when we suffer, or are exposed to the same miseries by a government, which we might expect in a country without government, our calamities is heightened by reflecting that we furnish the means by which we suffer!" ~ Thomas Paine, Common Sense

against any government action,' as well as the right of free speech. [*29]

In the 1760s, then-Governor of Massachusetts Francis Bernard and Lt. Governor/Chief Justice Thomas Hutchinson sought to shut down the Boston Gazette for its attacks on British policies.[30] [31] Given the benefit of hindsight, we can absolutely say that the Boston Gazette's speech was detrimental to the government and British society in Boston at the time. They tried numerous times to ban the publication under claims of libel, but Grand Juries continually rejected the case. They went to the Massachusetts House to get a ban passed legislatively. The Massachusetts House responded with a resolution passed that expressed support for the Boston Gazette.[†] [32]

Free expression was a relatively new right to be celebrated at the time. John Milton, an English author, helped lay the foundation to free speech when he

---

[*] "There is nothing so fretting and vexatious, nothing so justly terrible to tyrants, and their tools and abettors, as a free press." ~ Samuel Adams, The Boston Gazette

[†] "The Liberty of the Press is a great bulwark of the Liberty of the People: it is, therefore, the incumbent Duty of those who are constituted the Guardians of the People's Rights, to defend and maintain it." ~ The Massachusetts House, 1768

published Areopagitica[*][33] in 1644 as a response to Parliament's Ordinance for the Regulating of Printing which required all authors to be licensed by the government before they could print their works.[34] It hadn't been formally recognized into law until the British Bill of Rights in 1689 and, even then, it only officially extended to Parliament.[†][35]John Wilkes, a British Member of Parliament, became a celebrated hero in the UK and its colonies in the 1760s when the King tried to shut down his publication, "The North Briton," under the accusation of libel following its criticism of British policies.[36] The publication was full of harsh criticisms and satire, targeting the ruling elite of Great Britain.[37] "Wilkes and Liberty," became a rallying cry among British advocates for liberty in the 1760s. Wilkes most celebrated issue, North Briton #45, struck at the Monarchy directly.[‡][38] Attempts by King George III to

---

[*] "Give me the liberty to know, to utter, and to argue freely according to conscience, above all liberties." ~ John Milton

[†] "That the freedom of speech and debates or proceedings in Parliament ought not to be impeached or questioned in any court or place out of Parliament;" ~ British Bill of Rights, 1689

[‡] "The Stuart line has ever been intoxicated with the slavish doctrines of the absolute, independent, unlimited power of the crown. Some of that line were so weakly advised, as to endeavor to reduce them into practice: but the English nation was too spirited to suffer the least encroachment on the ancient liberties of this kingdom." ~ James Wilkes, North Briton #45 (1763)

shut down the publication and arrest John Wilkes for libel led to riots.[39] After copies of the publication were seized during an invasion of his home under general warrants, the case of John Wilkes not only helped set precedent for free speech in America but also for Due Process.[40]

The benefit governments get from shutting down free speech is clear. The publications were not just differential to the policies of government, but were hostile and undermined the very nature of government as it existed. The argument that rights only exist insofar as they benefit the existing status-quo would easily dismiss the right to be published in both cases if such an argument were reflective of the purpose and nature of rights. Contrary to this, rights exist as a boundary in the social contract limiting government action to protect our natural freedom.

Political speech wasn't the only protected speech in the eyes of our Founders. Our natural ability to express what we want to express extends to religion and many other aspects of life. Religious edicts had long been enforced by Parliament and the Monarchy prior to the United States, even instructing people on how to pray or conduct religious ceremonies. One such example also involving freedom of the Press is the Book of Common Prayer and the English Civil War of the 1640s.

One of the leading issues heading into the English Civil War of the 1640s was the authoritarian approach Charles I took towards religion.[41] This involved a significant attempt by Charles to reform the 'Book of Common Prayer,' which instructed Anglicans on how to worship. As head of the church, the Monarchy had established the Book of Common Prayer back during the English Reformation under Edward VI.[42] Charles sought to reform the book with a much more strict interpretation. By 1645, Parliament outlawed the Book of Common Prayer and replaced it with a, 'Directory of Public Worship,' which was much less widely used and even resented.[43]

Predating even this, some of the first settlers came to New England on the Mayflower in the 1620s driven by the desire for religious freedom.[44] [45] With Charles now imposing his new authoritarian approach on the Church of England, many Puritans followed the earlier Separatists in what became known as, "The Great Migration," in the 1630s.[46] [47] Far away from the reaches of Rome and Westminster Abbey, religion developed along a more democratic line in America. The motivations of protecting free expression in religion and politics reflect the culture of the Old World that early colonists were escaping, where the government had the ability to ban beliefs it saw as detrimental. The Founders were banning this from being practiced. To this day the

United Kingdom doesn't have an officially protected right to free speech even though it is very tolerant of speech.

Following the American Revolution, it yet again wasn't enough that the Constitution gave the people of America a democratically based government. The First Amendment was established in the Bill of Rights to ensure that the natural right to free expression would be tolerated even when the majority felt it was detrimental to the common good.[*] Contemporary calls to silence communists, fascists, or any other group or individual stand opposed to this foundation. As a natural right, free expression can never be justly taken away, only suppressed by oppressive powers.[†48] In the American Republic, rights exist as restraints against government specifically for when they're seen as detrimental.

---

[*] "Congress shall make no law respecting the establishment of religion, or prohibiting the free exercise thereof; or abridging the freedom of speech, or of the press, or the right of the people peaceably to assemble, and to petition the Government for a redress of grievances." ~ The First Amendment of the United States Constitution.

[†] "If men, through fear, fraud, or mistake, should in terms renounce or give up any essential natural right, the eternal law of reason and the grand end of society would absolutely vacate such renunciation. The right to freedom being the gift of God Almighty, it is not in the power of man to alienate this gift and voluntarily become a slave." ~ Samuel Adams, The Rights of the Colonists

The American Republic

Chapter 4: Due Process

> Due Process is the combination
> of these principles into law.

If we were to assume only the best of motivations for government and that the needs of society outweigh the needs of the individuals who populate it, Due Process wouldn't exist. It is a product of everything we've previously talked about from natural rights to consent of the governed and limitations of government's ability to act. Your natural right to freedom means there is a burden of proof to establish your guilt before punishment. Your natural rights to property and privacy mean the government must provide warranted reason before invading and searching your home or papers and private messages. The need to explain someone's rights when they're arrested and to provide them with a lawyer both limit the government's ability to prosecute with impunity. Jury rights ensure that the people themselves are granting consent to the law attempting to be enforced. If the government breaks the rules of Due Process, the case itself is thrown entirely out of court. All of these things limit the ability of government to act and protect our natural freedom.

The 1760s case of John Wilkes was thrown out by the British courts because North Briton 45 was seized from his personal property under an illegal warrant granting a general search of his property.[49] This was not an isolated incident, but a continued tradition of British and American law. [*50] The Magna Carta was first authored by Roman Catholic Archbishop Stephen Langton in 1215.[51] The famous document outlined a number of rights for British citizens such as trial by jury; requiring trustworthy testimony; and Habeas Corpus, the

---

[*] "I have now taken notice of everything that has been urged upon the present point, and, upon the whole, we are all of opinion that the warrant to seize and carry away the party's papers in the case of a seditious libel is illegal and void." ~ Lord Camden, Entick v. Carrington and Three Other King's Messengers

"The principles laid down in this opinion affect the very essence of constitutional liberty and security. They reach farther than the concrete form of the case then before the court, with its adventitious circumstances; they apply to all invasions on the part of the government and its employees of the sanctity of a man's home and the privacies of life. It is not the breaking of his doors and the rummaging of his drawers that constitutes the essence of the offence, but it is the invasion of his indefeasible right of personal security, personal liberty, and private property, where that right has never been forfeited by his conviction of some public offence -- it is the invasion of this sacred right which underlies and constitutes the essence of Lord Camden's judgment." ~ Justice Bradley, Lead Opinion: Boyd v. United States 1886

concept that no one can be imprisoned unlawfully.[*52] Later on, in 1679, the concept of Habeas Corpus was expanded with the Habeas Corpus Act.[53] The British Bill of Rights in 1689 expanded Due Process following the Glorious Revolution.[54] This bill further recognized Due Process rights by banning excessive bail and preventing fines or seizures before someone was convicted.[†55]

As part of the Sugar Act of 1764, Great Britain entrusted enforcement of the law to military courts with

---

[*] "In future no official shall place a man on trial upon his own unsupported statement, without producing credible witnesses to the truth of it." ~ Magna Carta Clause 38

"No free man shall be seized or imprisoned, or stripped of his rights or possessions, or outlawed or exiled, or deprived of his standing in any way, nor will we proceed with force against him, or send others to do so, except by the lawful judgment of his equals or by the law of the land." ~ Magna Carta Clause 39

"To no one will we sell, to no one deny or delay right or justice." ~ Magna Carta Clause 40

[†] "That excessive bail ought not to be required, nor excessive fines imposed, nor cruel and unusual punishments inflicted; That jurors ought to be duly impanelled and returned, and jurors which pass upon men in trials for high treason ought to be freeholders; That all grants and promises of fines and forfeitures of particular persons before conviction are illegal and void;" ~ English Bill of Rights 1689

juries in America.[56] [57] This became a greatly expanded practice by the British government as colonial jurors rejected enforcement of laws and taxes over which they had no say by refusing to declare people guilty of breaking laws to which they did not consent. As time passed, the military courts started transporting prisoners to stand trial in England away from their peers. One of the actions of the first Continental Congress in 1774 was to pass a resolution calling on the colonies to offer armed resistance to these practices.[*][58] The Declaration of Independence passed later by the Second Continental Congress listed these actions as part of the illegal actions by the King, among others.[†][59] They cited this among the offenses knowing that colonial jurors were declaring 'guilty' people free.

Following the American Revolution, and the Articles of Confederation, the United States Constitution secured some of these Due Process rights in 1787.[60] It guaranteed Habeas Corpus except in cases of invasion or rebellion. It prevented the legislature from passing laws

---

[*] "[T]he seizing, or attempting to seize, any person in America, in order to transport such person beyond the sea, for trial of offenses, committed within the body of a country in America, being against a law, will justify, and ought to meet with resistance and reprisal." ~ The First Continental Congress, 1774

[†] "For depriving us, in many Cases, of the Benefits of Trial by Jury: For transporting us beyond Seas to be tried for pretended Offences:" ~ The Declaration of Independence

declaring people guilty without a trial. It prevented the government from punishing someone for doing something that was legal at the time they did it, but is no longer legal.[61] The original Constitution also guaranteed the right to a jury in all criminal trials. It guarantees a trial in the State where the crime allegedly took place.[62] The original Constitution echoed the Magna Carta by requiring at least two witnesses for trials of treason and it prevented anyone from being considered guilty just because they are related to a traitor.[63] These provisions provided the start to Due Process in America, but some felt they didn't go far enough in protecting the people from the government.

Two years later Congress passed the Bill of Rights. Provisions within the Bill of Rights required the government to obtain a warrant before invading a person's property or information; vastly expanded the right to a Jury trial; prevented people from being tried for the same crime repeatedly; prevented someone from being forced to testify against themselves; and promised Due Process before Life, Liberty or Property can be taken. The Bill of Rights promised a right to speedy trial; knowledge of whose accusing you of something; as well as the right to an attorney and a chance to prepare your defense. It also banned excessive bails, fines, and punishments, and promised compensation in cases of public domain. Of the ten amendments to the

Constitution in the Bill of Rights, half of the Amendments were designed to protect Due Process. On top of these, the 9th Amendment served as a vague clause protecting any rights they hadn't considered. All the amendments placed limitations on the government's ability to take action.

The limitations within the Constitution and the Bill of Rights were put in place by the generation of Americans that had just removed a King and replaced him with a Constitutional Republic and democratic processes. Due Process wasn't simply a means of ensuring someone was guilty before they could be punished. It was a means of limiting the ability of the government to prosecute its case and it ensured that such a case could only be prosecuted with the consent of the governed. This doesn't make sense if we assume the government has the best of intentions and that the needs of society outweigh the rights of individuals. It requires that we recognize rights as being a natural state of freedom for all individuals, restraining the government in what actions it can take outside the protection of that natural freedom, and that it can only take such actions with the consent of the governed. In the American Republic, Due Process is the combination of these principles into law.

The American Republic

Chapter 5: The Right to Bear Arms

> There are times when individuals must defend their rights with lethal force, even against the government.

The establishment of government is recognition that force is necessary and appropriate in defense of our rights. As established with the necessity of recognizing and securing rights, government alone cannot be trusted with such a monopoly of power. The philosophy behind America recognized that when all formal appeals to government have failed, the people have a right to appeal above the authority of government through means of force.[*][64] People have a natural right to overthrow their government in defense of their rights. The Declaration of Independence made this case as the very basis for the formation of America and one cannot be an American

---

[*] "Wherever law ends, tyranny begins, if the law be transgressed to another's harm; and whosoever in authority exceeds the power given him by the law, and makes use of the force he has under his command, to compass that upon the subject, which the law allows not, ceases in that to be a magistrate; and, acting without authority, may be opposed, as any other man, who by force invades the right of another." ~ John Locke, Second Treatise of Government

without acknowledging the validity of their cause.* The ultimate check against tyranny is an armed citizenry prepared to meet force with force. The right to bear arms is a natural and universal means of preserving our rights against thugs and tyrants alike.

Having violated the rights of their subjects, the British Government violated its purpose as a government and justified the need for the colonials to become independent. However, the American Revolution did not begin with the Declaration of Independence in 1776. The American Republic began with the militias of New England resisting arms confiscation on April 19th, 1775.[65] [66] Prior to this first battle of the revolution the Military Governor of Massachusetts, Thomas Gage, tried to reduce the arms accessible to the colonists[67] and King George III supplemented this by banning the import of guns and ammunition in 1774.[68] As part of these efforts, General Gage deployed troops and seized cannons from

---

* "Prudence, indeed, will dictate that Governments long established should not be changed for light and transient causes; and accordingly all experience hath shown, that mankind are more disposed to suffer, while evils are sufferable, than to right themselves by abolishing the forms to which they are accustomed. But when a long train of abuses and usurpations, pursuing invariably the same Object evinces a design to reduce them under absolute Despotism, it is their right, it is their duty, to throw off such Government, and to provide new Guards for their future security." ~ The Declaration of Independence

colonial militias in September of 1774 in an event that is now known as the Powder Alarm.[69] [70] In response to this confiscation, Paul Revere formed a spy network to watch British troop movements and ensure that the people of New England could hide their arms if the British tried to march on other stockpiles.[71] That December, the colonials received faulty intelligence that the British were planning on moving their own cannon and powder out of a poorly defended fort in Portsmouth, New Hampshire. Acting swiftly, New Hampshire militias overwhelmed the fort and stole muskets, powder and cannon for the defense of the colonies.[72] [73] Another notable incident which nearly started the revolution was the Salem Alarm in February of 1775, also known as Leslie's Retreat, when British regulars were sent to seize arms being stored in Salem, Massachusetts. Thanks to the spy networks set up by Paul Revere, colonial militias received enough notice to stall the British troops and move their stores of arms to another location.[74] [75] [76]

The colonists were resisting the British government's attempts to confiscate arms because they believed in an armed civilian population and in their natural right to revolution if their peaceful appeals failed. The First Continental Congress even endorsed a call on the colonies to take up arms in case their peaceful appeals failed.[*][77] [78] The Congress didn't invent this tradition of the English militia, but were continuing it. The ancient Anglo-Saxons predating the Norman Invasion required all able-bodied free men to form militias called "fyrds," if called upon.[79] The Assize of Arms in 1181 required all freemen to own arms in case the King needed to call upon the militia.[80] [81] In 1363, Edward III banned generic sports and required people practice archery in order to keep the militia of Great Britain prepared for war.[82] [83] The British Bill of Rights in 1689 recognized the individual right to own arms for every Protestant.[†][84] The English colonies even utilized this tradition to their advantage during the French and Indian War and many of the responding minutemen on April 19th were veterans of that conflict.[85]

Following the revolution, the Articles of Confederation required States to keep formal militias and the Constitution originally limited appropriation for

---

[*] "[W]e, therefore, for the honour, defence and security of this county and province, advise, [...] that the inhabitants of those towns and districts, who are qualified, do use their utmost diligence to acquaint themselves with the art of war as soon as possible, and do, for that purpose, appear under arms at least once every week." ~ Joseph Warren, the Suffolk Resolves

[†] "That the subjects which are Protestants may have arms for their defence suitable to their conditions and as allowed by law;" ~ The British Bill of Rights

any standing army to two years and gave the Congress the power to create militias to serve the government as well as giving the President command over such militias when called upon.* Modern advocates for gun control often assert the second amendment was about government endorsed militias and government control over what the people may have in terms of arms. If they were correct there would be no need for the Second Amendment in the Bill of Rights because this already exists in the Constitution. Instead, like the other amendments of the Bill of Rights, the Second Amendment recognized the natural individual right of "the people" to own weapons and stated that the

---

* "[…]To provide for calling forth the Militia to execute the Laws of the Union, suppress Insurrections and repel Invasions; To provide for organizing, arming, and disciplining, the Militia, and for governing such Part of them as may be employed in the Service of the United States, reserving to the States respectively, the Appointment of the Officers, and the Authority of training the Militia according to the discipline prescribed by Congress;" ~ United States Constitution, Article 1 Section 8

"The President shall be Commander in Chief of the Army and Navy of the United States, and of the Militia of the several States, when called into the actual Service of the United States;" ~ United States Constitution, Article 2 Section 2

government could not limit their ability to own weapons.[*]

The express purpose of the Second Amendment, cited within the amendment itself, is both for the security and liberty of the people. It is both for personal security and for political liberty in design so the American people can defend themselves from thugs and tyrants alike. In introducing the Bill of Rights to the Congress to be adopted, James Madison spoke on the matter himself and cited the intent of each of the amendments. In that original proposal, Madison worded the amendment in a much more straightforward fashion. He originally proposed, "The right of the people to keep and bear arms shall not be infringed; a well armed and well regulated militia being the best security of a free country; but no person religiously scrupulous of bearing arms shall be compelled to render military service in person."[86] This cites the clear intent of the amendment as being for the people. That intent cannot be lost when the proposal is read in full. Madison lists this as part of a much larger, singular amendment designed to be placed in the Constitution as a list of individual rights. Over the course of debate that singular amendment, and others he

_____

[*] "A well regulated Militia, being necessary to the security of a free State, the right of the people to keep and bear Arms, shall not be infringed." ~ The Second Amendment

proposed, were separated into the ten amendments we know today as the Bill of Rights.

The right to bear arms comes from the English heritage of the American colonies. It was the last right exercised by the English subjects of America when all others had been ignored. It was the first right exercised by the American people as a necessary measure to secure their liberty. It exists not to the benefit of the government, but as an obstruction of the government's ability to act against the people and it secures the means of the people to act against the government if all other appeals fail. In the American Republic, there are times when individuals must defend their rights with lethal force, even against the government.

The American Republic

Chapter 6: State's Rights

> Government loses consent as it
> gets further from the people.

Faced with the challenge of forming a new nation based on their principles, the Founders had to establish a practical form of government derived from those principles and designed to protect them. The Articles of Confederation were the effective government of the United States following the Declaration of Independence and functioned well when the States faced a common enemy. Following the revolution, States focused more on their own interests and so a faction of the Founders formed the Federalist convention in the hopes of drafting a government that would better unite the nation.

A small portion of the members of the Federalist convention went so far as to try and eliminate the very existence of the States under the Constitution and place all government under a popular legislature. Other members recognized a necessary role for the States in the national government in order for there to be unity behind its formation.* [87] Some members of the convention also refused to support any government

---

* See end notes.

which encroached on State sovereignty, proving the point. Going back to the first proposed draft of the Constitution, there was always the design to have two parts to the legislature but there was much debate as to how these would be formed and why. When the Senate was chosen to be a body reflecting the States, the question arose of whether the States should be represented equally in the Senate or if the number of Senators should be reflective of the population or property to be taxed within each state.[88] The compromise struck became more successful than any of those in the convention could have imagined.

The Congress divided into two legislatures: The House and the Senate. The House would represent the people directly. The Senate would represent the State governments equally. The House alone, being representative of the people direct, had the power of taxation under the condition that such taxation would be implemented in a way that was proportionate to each State's representation in the Congress. This linked taxation and representation not only in giving the power of taxation solely to the people, but also ensuring that those with more say in those taxes would be paying more of the taxes they supported. New York, for example, easily had more say in the implementation of taxes than a smaller state such as New Hampshire. As such, the consent of the people of New York mattered more than that of the people of New Hampshire in passing the tax through the legislature. It only made sense, then, that the people of New York be more responsible for those taxes they push through.

The Senate would be chosen by the State governments. The Senate's consent was necessary for any bill passed by the House (and vice-versa). The Senate's consent was necessary for the President to make appointments to various positions in the government, the courts, and for ambassadors. The Senate's consent was also required for foreign treaties. If the House were to vote for an impeachment, the Senate was made responsible for carrying out the impeachment process and rendering a verdict. The end result of this Congressional formation was that while both the Senate and the House had the power to create bills, the House was given unique powers of starting actions such as taxes, budgets, and impeachments whereas the Senate's unique powers were a checking influence against growth and abuse of power within the Federal government's operations.

While the form of the Congress created under the Constitution was a compromise between a number of camps, that compromise resulted in a better application of their principles than any single group's proposals. Part of the reason the Constitution was able to be ratified at all was because of its recognition of the States. There were two political parties vying for power under the Articles of Confederation: The Nationalists and the Federalists. The Nationalists wanted a stronger central government than the Articles while the Federalists supported the current confederated government. This flipped with the introduction of the Constitution as the Nationalists, who actually proposed it, renamed themselves the 'Federalists,' and marketed their government as still being a tiered system with recognition of State sovereignty. The previous, "Federalists," were then rebranded as, "Antifederalists," under this marketing.[89] [90]

Antifederalists are less talked about today since the Constitution was ratified, but their members played an essential role in winning America's freedom from England, curtailing the Federal tier's power, and shaping the Constitution. Notable Antifederalists include Samuel Adams, Thomas Jefferson, Patrick Henry, Richard Henry Lee, and more. They not only ensured that America would remain a country of united States instead of a central government, but also that there were recognized rights placed in the Constitution after it was ratified. The debate and context surrounding the Federalists and the Antifederalists was ultimately about what government best reflects the principles previously discussed in this book. What form of government best protects our natural rights with our consent?

James Madison, who authored the first draft of the Constitution, attempted to balance the concerns of those who wanted a Federal Government strong enough to unite Americans and the concerns of those who felt government closer to the people was more effective at representing them. Madison's solution was to list the specific function of the Federal Government within the Constitution itself so that all other matters would be entirely left to more local forms of government.[*91] This list of powers granted to the Federal tier survived the convention and remains in the Constitution today in Article 1, Section 8.[†92] [93] [94] By placing this list into the Constitution, James Madison helped fulfill John Locke's view of the limited social contract and negated Hobbes view of nearly unlimited power for the government. Madison felt so strongly about this principle that following the ratification of the Constitution, he

---

[*] "Mr. MADISON said, that he had brought with him into the Convention a strong bias in favor of an enumeration and definition of the powers necessary to be exercised by the National Legislature; but had also brought doubts concerning its practicability." ~ Journal of the Federal Convention, May 31st, 1787.

[†] " The Congress shall have Power To lay and collect Taxes, Duties, Imposts and Excises, to pay the Debts and provide for the common Defence and general Welfare of the United States; but all Duties, Imposts and Excises shall be uniform throughout the United States; To [...]" ~ United States Constitution, Article 1, Section 8

Additional quote from James Madison in endnotes.

proposed the 10th Amendment of the Bill of Rights with the intent of ensuring that no power unlisted in the Constitution be presumed to exist for the Federal Government.^{*95 96}

By limiting the Federal government's role and leaving the States in charge of solving matters pertaining to law, education, healthcare, conservation, social safety nets, etc., the Constitution didn't just ensure that people would have a better proportion of representation in government. This also ensured that the amount of people who did not consent to their government would be minimal. This can be demonstrated in three models.

In the First Model: There is a country of 100 people that is a direct democracy. In a controversial vote about any given issue, fifty-one people can force an undesired government on the other forty nine. This leaves forty-nine people under a government to which they did not consent.

In the Second Model: A country of the same size has five States of twenty people. If each of these States has jurisdiction on the controversial issue and votes for their own solution, the division will leave eleven people forcing an undesired government on the other nine. The total number of

---

[*] "The powers not delegated to the United States by the Constitution, nor prohibited by it to the States, are reserved to the States respectively, or to the people." ~ The Tenth Amendment

people not consenting to the government in the country as a whole will be forty-five.

In the Third Model: A country of the same size has ten States of ten people. If each of these States votes on the matter, six people will be forcing four others into an undesired government. The total number of people not consenting to the government they are under in this country has now fallen to forty.

If we were to apply these models to the scale of the United States with recognition of the divisions that exist in how to address any given topic, we find entire sections of country would be unrepresentative of their population in a national democracy. By dividing the nation into States which can determine how to address these issues, we ensure people continue to have a say in the government of the land. By requiring a three-fourths majority to amend the Constitution and limiting the Federal tier's jurisdiction to that three-fourths approval, the Founders left in place a document that was to ensure a greater consent of the governed so long as this limitation was followed. The people in any given region only retain a voice in government when that region retains its sovereignty. In the American Republic, government loses consent as it gets further from the people.

The American Republic

Chapter 7: The American Democracy

> Progressivism is a rejection of the American Republic and the embrace of an entirely different working philosophy.

The American Republic looked at rights as a natural fact. We're naturally free and capable of acting on our own for our own interests. People band together and form governments to ensure protection of this natural freedom. Governments that fail to recognize this natural freedom, violate it, or operate without the consent of the governed are not legitimate. The people have a duty to overthrow such institutions with the purpose of forming a new government in order to protect their natural freedom. Rights chartered by government were not to be seen as the creation of such freedom, but the acknowledgement of government's purpose to protect it above all else. This acknowledgement serves as boundaries set specifically against government action and violation of such boundaries violates the justification of government's existence in the first place. Government was seen as an evil by the Founders due to the fact that it had to be upheld with force and that evil was only tolerable so long as it existed constrained and acted with consent for the intended purpose of protecting individual rights. Government is less reflective of the people the greater the scale of its implementation. This was the foundation for the American philosophy and the American Republic. Progressivism is a rejection of all these things.

While the American Republic sought to secure rights for all individuals as recognition of natural fact, the Progressive movement begins its foundation of rights based on what it thinks individuals should do with their freedom for what they see as the public interest.[*][97] Where the American Republic's vision of rights limited the government, the Progressive movement's case sought to promote its expansion and invasion into the natural rights for the 'collective good.'[†][98] The Progressives argue that to live in society requires the

---

[*] "This country belongs to the people who inhabit it. Its resources, its business, its institutions and its laws should be utilized, maintained or altered in whatever manner will best promote the general interest. It is time to set the public welfare in the first place." ~ Progressive Platform of 1912

[†] "We grudge no man a fortune in civil life if it is honorably obtained and well used. It is not even enough that it should have been gained without doing damage to the community. We should permit it to be gained only so long as the gaining represents benefit to the community. This, I know, implies a policy of a far more active governmental interference with social and economic conditions in this country than we have yet had, but I think we have got to face the fact that such an increase in governmental control is now necessary." ~ Theodore Roosevelt, Founder of the Progressive Party

consent of society, as represented by government, rather than the government requiring consent of the people as individuals. The Progressive philosophy was on the rise in America before Theodore Roosevelt, the first Progressive President, but its foundation established itself as the dominant political philosophy between Theodore Roosevelt and Franklin D. Roosevelt in a period known as 'The Progressive Era.'

The death of the American Republic was from a two-pronged attack. The first blow was the 16th Amendment to the Constitution in 1913.[*99] This amendment separated taxation from representation by eliminating the enumeration requirement in taxes. Enumeration required that taxes be distributed among the American people in proportion to the amount of Representatives they had in the House. States with more Representatives, who had more say in what spending occurred, no longer had to bear the burden of that spending. With the 16th Amendment, the government could now place the cost of its expenditures on people who had minority representation. The 16th Amendment created a system where little regard exists for the cost of

---

[*] "The Congress shall have power to lay and collect taxes on incomes, from whatever source derived, without apportionment among the several States, and without regard to any census or enumeration." ~ The Sixteenth Amendment

government as it is to be paid by the minority rather than the majority in control.

The second blow came two months later with the 17th Amendment.[*][100] This amendment targeted State Suffrage in the Senate by eliminating the ability of State Governments to choose their own Senators to represent them. With the 17th Amendment, Senators became responsible to the People direct, bypassing State legislatures, and effectively replacing the representative body of the States within the Constitution with an alternative body also representing the people like the House. Before this change, bills required the consent of State governments and thus were less likely to trample on the authority of local governments. The original Senate was to protect local sovereignty which kept government closer to the governed. Since this change a bill that might appropriate funding for highways, for example, is now likely to pass with provisions requiring State governments to adopt standards such as drinking age limits or seatbelt laws to receive the funding. Without State suffrage, the national government takes precedent over local voices in both big population and

---

[*] "The Senate of the United States shall be composed of two Senators from each State, elected by the people thereof for six years; and each Senator shall have one vote. The electors in each State shall have the qualifications requisite for electors of the most numerous branch of the State legislatures. [...]" ~ The Seventeenth Amendment

little population areas instead of a system where the central authority could only pass measures, appoint judges, enter treaties, etc. with the consent of the local peoples of America.

The combination of these two amendments is a less representative body enacting law without care to the cost. Entire sections of the country may be forced to live under dictated law by a majority comprised entirely of people who do not live where these laws are to be enforced. The representative government on the local level is powerless to stop it. With these two amendments, the American Republic, comprised of united States, gave way to a new American Democracy that operated on a new foundation based on Progressive philosophy.

This new American Democracy was only the first step of the Progressive movement. Their goal was to nullify the social contract of the Constitution and to render its limitations of Federal power obsolete so they could enforce a government empowered to reach into the lives of Americans and mold them into whatever the predominant Progressive class desired.*[101] [102] During the transition phase into the American Democracy, it was still necessary to pass Constitutional amendments in

---

* See endnotes.

order to take actions designed to accomplish this goal. The 18th Amendment's necessity to give the Federal government the power to prohibit the sale of alcohol was due to the fact that the country was still transitioning into this Progressive Democracy in 1919.[*103] Early laws targeting narcotics emerged under the guise of the new Federal power to tax without enumeration.[104] Marijuana was soon after also targeted under the guise of the power to tax.[105] As the Progressive philosophy transitioned to the dominant political force these measures, originally created under a consented legal authority to tax through the social contract of the Constitution, became Federal bans without amendment granting such authority. They are just two examples of a massive trend in how the government's operation shifted over the past century from a limited entity requiring consent of the governed to an empowered institution that now requires small majorities to enlarge and supermajorities to restrict or shrink.

Progressives exist in both the cultural right and counter-culture left in America today due to its longstanding history in the American government over

---

[*] "After one year from the ratification of this article the manufacture, sale, or transportation of intoxicating liquors within, the importation thereof into, or the exportation thereof from the United States and all territory subject to the jurisdiction thereof for beverage purposes is hereby prohibited." ~ The Eighteenth Amendment, Section One

the past century. Progressives often cite their philosophy as being built off of the philosophy of the Founding Fathers and the American Republic, but they reject the foundational philosophies presented in this book. Where the natural freedom of the American Republic meant you had the ability to take action and the government was limited in stopping you, the American Democracy justifies restriction of freedom based on an inability to trust individuals to act in a manner that benefits society. Speech that was once recognized as being protected is now banned if it's seen as being negative to society. Weapons, once seen as a natural way to defend oneself and thus a protected freedom, now require justification to own and face restrictions over theoretical abuse. Warrants that required justification of the government's ability to invade your right to privacy are now seen as obstacles to be ignored when inconvenient. Juries originally designed as a method of maintaining consent of the governed are now instructed to uphold the written law regardless of their personal consent to it. Powers that used to be left to the States and the People by default are assumed to be within the grasp of the Federal government. The American Democracy has even given way to the belief that government action itself is to be considered a right. Progressivism is a rejection of the American Republic and the embrace of an entirely different working philosophy.

The American Republic

Chapter 8: The American Oligarchy

> The American Democracy itself is in decay and only a restoration of the Republic can save us from an Oligarchy.

The American Republic lasted over a century between 1789 and 1913. The American Democracy has been in place for roughly a century in its own right. That period is coming to an end. Without the Constitutional process of restricting the Federal government's actions and growth, the American Democracy has grown numerous agencies which have imposed regulations with only the vaguest of permissions granted by Congress and largely without the consent of the governed. The political process has deviated from a method of achieving agreement within society before moving forward to a method of winning narrow elections and using such victories as an excuse to dictate law through technical processes. The result of this has been a growing partisan divide within the population.[106] With less of a need to convince the American people before acting, and more of an impasse forming within the population, we see the natural tendency arising where Americans want the Federal tier to act without permission of the States and for the President to act when the Congress is in deadlock. As these trends take hold, Americans are slipping from their empowered and cancerous democratic government into a new American Oligarchy.

If the Progressive Democracy's foundation is the removal of natural rights and the establishment of a government empowered to act on behalf of the narrowest of majorities, the new American Oligarchy's foundation seems to be the common cry to action in haste in the face of lacking consensus. It is not enough that the rules restricting government action to widespread consent of the governed have been removed because now the narrow majorities which hold power are so far apart in philosophy that no middle ground can be reached. Rather than taking this as a sign that our government has outpaced permission of its citizens to take what actions it has, most Americans see scapegoats to blame for obstructing their clear singular path forward. No one who has actively debated politics with fellow Americans can realistically deny that the left and the right see opposite solutions to the same identified problems and yet Americans seem to consistently cite lobbyists and long-standing politicians as the problem rather than those neighbors with which they disagree. Even when the disagreement is acknowledged, it only seems to serve the cry to action without consent even more because it feels as if no consensus could ever be achieved.

When the Progressive Era first started, Congress replaced the Constitution as the definitive power granting government permission to act. As the American Oligarchy takes hold, the Congress has turned alarming amounts of power over to the agencies of the United States. Where Congress was once the body that had to debate and shape law, with specific limitations under the Constitution, Congress now issues general directives for Federal Agencies to form regulatory laws that are often changed with the wave of the President's pen depending on singular elections.[*][107] [108] So extensive are these laws by agencies that no singular person or small team of people can honestly know them.[109]

Another example of the transition to an Oligarchy is the transition of War Powers. In the American Republic, Congress alone had sole authority in offensive military actions. Contemporaries often cite

---

[*] "Over the course of the last century, but especially since the 1930s and then ramping up since the 1960s, a whole lot of the responsibility in this body has been kicked to a bunch of alphabet soup bureaucracies. All the acronyms that people know about their government or don't know about their government are the places where most actual policymaking, kind of in a way, lawmaking is happening right now. [...] And so, what we mostly do around this body is not pass laws. What we mostly do is decide to give permission to the Secretary or the administrator of bureaucracy X, Y, or Z to make law-like regulations. That's mostly what we do here." ~ Senator Ben Sasse

history out of context to try and rewrite this fact, but what power the President had to act unilaterally was solely a reactive power to direct attacks and not some abstract 'defense' by taking offensive action.[*][110][111][112][113][114] It wasn't until the late Republic and the American Democracy that a power to take unilateral action, without it being a direct response to being attacked first, was placed under the Presidency.[115] Like with the regulatory authority, the justification for needing this power to attack first without debate was a cry for haste

---

[*] "The constitution vests the power of declaring war in Congress; therefore no offensive expedition of importance can be undertaken until after they shall have deliberated upon the subject and authorized such a measure." ~ George Washington, 1793

"The constitution supposes, what the History of all Governments demonstrates, that the Executive is the branch of power most interested in war, and most prone to it. It has accordingly with studied care vested the question of war to the Legislature." ~ James Madison, 1798

"Considering that Congress alone is constitutionally invested with the power of changing our condition from peace to war, I have thought it my duty to await their authority for using force in any degree which could be avoided." ~ Thomas Jefferson, 1805

"The President shall be Commander in Chief of the Army and Navy of the United States, and of the Militia of the several States, **when called into the actual Service of the United States**; [...]" ~ US Constitution Article 1, Section 2 (Emphasis Added)

See endnotes for additional quote from Alexander Hamilton.

and because of the possibility that the People may not consent to the action. Like with regulatory agencies, the ability of government to act militarily has been placed beneath the Presidency.

The ability of the Executive and its agency branches to act unilaterally has already begun to degrade into uncontrolled unilateral actions. In 2016, the Central Intelligence Agency, a branch of government formed without Constitutional Amendment, spied on members of Congress who were considered political dissidents to its agenda.[116] [117] [118] [119] When it was caught doing so, no repercussions came to the CIA or its then-Director John Brennan. Likewise, the National Security Agency has dropped all semblance of respecting the warrant system and has collected private records from Americans indiscriminately. When questioned about the matter, then-Director James Clapper lied to Congress about the fact that they were doing it until it was revealed by leaked documents that the NSA was, in fact, violating the privacy of Americans.[120] [121] After this Clapper stated that he had been mistaken and faced no repercussions while the leaker, Edward Snowden, was forced to flee the country or face imprisonment without a jury trial.[122] [123]

The incidents have not been isolated. The Drug Enforcement Agency also ignored warrants and began spying on Americans in 1994 with its Special Operations

Division which was comprised of a task force including the FBI, CIA, NSA, IRS and eventually the Department of Homeland Security. This unit not only spied on Americans illegally, but hid the fact that they were doing so by placing anonymous tips to local police in order to hide the illegal source of the information.[124] In another case, the Bureau of Alcohol, Tobacco, Firearms and Explosives (BATF) was caught embezzling cash through illegal operations and using those funds to bypass Congressional oversight and appropriations. When the program was discovered, the Justice Department attempted to cover up the slush fund rather than bring the revelations to Congress.[125] The BATF also ran an operation of purposefully selling weapons to drug cartels while using the results to push for more regulations against firearms in America.[126] These are just some of the examples of how agencies of the American Democracy are acting without consent of the governed as America moves towards an Oligarchy status.

The decay of the American Democracy into an Oligarchy is natural for a democracy as big as the United States. Unlike the Republic, which delineated authority towards the individual, in the American Democracy power flows upwards and the reliance on agencies grows because of the vast differences of views held across the States of America. As more people fall under its jurisdiction, governmental actions hold less consent because there are more dissenting opinions about how things should be done. As we separate the responsibility of paying for what we vote for, it's natural that the government becomes less accountable for how the money is spent. As we become more concerned with our security than our freedom, it's natural that we lose both our security and our freedom from the government. The Republic's transition to a Democracy significantly deteriorated the People's consent and representation in government. The American Democracy itself is in decay and only a restoration of the Republic can save us from an Oligarchy.

We need to recognize that…

Rights are natural, they are universal, and they are a fundamental necessity to valid government.

All valid government requires consent of the governed.

Rights exist as restraints against government specifically for when they're seen as detrimental.

Due Process is the combination of American principles into law.

There are times when individuals must defend their rights with lethal force, even against the government.

Government loses consent as it gets further from the people.

Progressivism is a rejection of the American Republic and the embrace of an entirely different working philosophy.

The American Philosophy is decaying and only a restoration of the Republic can save us from an Oligarchy.

The American Republic

Epilogue

The principles of the American Revolution are rare and unique to this country. These principles have driven constant debate and even war among the American people over the course of our history including the current tensions of today. Identifying and defining these principles again is necessary for any reconciliation. If no reconciliation can be found among the American people in identifying our common social contract, then nature will drive us continually further apart until subjugation or separation takes place.

Our bias to what is happening today is the belief that the United States will always be one nation and that there is no possibility that this could deteriorate into occupation of sections of the country or that we could possibly break into a plurality because no consensus could be reached. Historically we can look and see that this is not the case. The United States has already previously occupied our own territory after an attempt of separation over the issue of slavery and State's Rights. There are a great many more countries that exist today than in the past. In 1900 the number of sovereign nations was in the 70s. Today that number is closer to 200. The tendency is to believe that human beings will find some uniform conformity of principles that will unite us into one larger nation. This was possible in the past of the American Republic because there was a unity of principles under which to unite.

The establishment of a national democracy above the States eroded those principles by emphasizing where our differences lie as the government centralized. Where before we were States united by our few common principles, today we are States under a larger body that sets policies the States must follow. Each policy where the People dissent from each other becomes a division amongst us as a whole instead of differences between different States. As our differences become emphasized under one central government, the government becomes less effective in representing us since we all want different things. As the government has become less effective, we have begun to call for greater autonomy of the government outside of our legislative process. Our government is seen as no longer representing us because of our differences and because we have turned over increasingly greater authority to agencies outside of our representation.

What remains is the view that some great American awakening will occur where, 'the People,' (insert meant agenda of choice) will rise up and institute overwhelming democratic victories that will reform the system. The notion that this author holds is that it is the people themselves who have abandoned the principles of our Republic and are now abandoning the principles of our Democracy. If this is the case, no such mass reform is likely or possible. What will occur is the government will swing in greater and greater movements, back and forth, with each majority won. When majorities are not won, the situation will serve as a call to centralize more authority under government bureaucracies who may act with the vaguest of permissions by the legislature. This is based off an observation of what is currently happening in the United States today.

If that analysis is correct, the question arises: How can anyone seriously believe that the United States will continue to remain one nation? The basis of that status quo relies on either the previously mentioned hope that some democratic awakening is around the corner, a hope that diminishes as democracy itself erodes, or by virtue of pure force alone. This latter possibility is horrific but also unlikely to succeed in the long run. The United States is too vast a nation and too well armed to police under authority that lacks unified support. Such a conflict would likely see a breaking of the United States into regions that have enough consensus to rule by force within themselves but unable to expand into neighboring territories until they have consolidated power.

If correct, the choice Americans face is not a question of whether power will be returned to localized forms of government but rather what that transition and end result will look like. Will we peacefully acknowledge our differences and work together as States united, or will we deny our differences and subject whom we can through conflict? A nation requires unifying principles under which we all live and support. What will those principles be and how will we find them? The author hopes they can be the rarely appreciated recognition of Individual Rights and that this book serves the purpose of finding that recognition and avoiding such a conflict. If a conflict should occur, the author hopes that these will be the principles to prevail. They are worth killing and dying over today as much as they were in the past. Live free or die; death is not the worst of evils.

Chapter One

[1] Jefferson, Thomas. Letter. "Writing of The Declaration of Independence." *America, Vol.3*, p.166–p.170. Cited in the US Constitution Coach Kit. Franklin, TN: PowerThink Publishing, 2009. Electronic.

[2] Richardson, Edward W. *Standards and Colors of the American Revolution*. University of Pennsylvania Press and the Pennsylvania Society of Sons of the Revolution and Its Color Guard, 1982. <https://www.crwflags.com/fotw/flags/us-wacr.html>

[3] Ibid.

[4] Otis, James. "In Opposition to the Writs of Assistance." 1761. *The World's Famous Orations, Vol.8*, p.27-36. Cited in the US Constitution Coach Kit. Franklin, TN: PowerThink Publishing, 2009. Electronic.

[5] Ibid.

[6] Otis, James. "The Rights of the British Colonies Asserted and Proved." 1764. *Pamphlets of the American Revolution 1750-1776, p.439-440*. The Belknap Press of Harvard University Press, 1965. Harvard College Library. <https://www.pbs.org/wgbh/aia/part2/2h18.html>

[7] Jefferson, Thomas. Paul Leicester Ford, ed. *The Writings of Thomas Jefferson*. New York: G. P. Putnam's Sons, 1892, p.373–381. <https://www.encyclopediavirginia.org/Thomas_Jefferson_s_Argument_in_Howell_v_Netherland_1770>

[8] Jefferson, Thomas. "Jefferson's Original Draft of the Declaration." *America, Vol. 3*, p.171-179. Cited in the US Constitution Coach Kit. Franklin, TN: PowerThink Publishing, 2009. Electronic.

[9] Lincoln, Abraham. "Peoria Speech." 1854. Neely, Mark E. Jr. 1982. *The Abraham Lincoln Encyclopedia*. New York: Da Capo Press, Inc. < https://www.nps.gov/liho/learn/historyculture/peoriaspeech.htm>

[10] Douglass, Frederick. "Speech on the Dredd Scott Decision." 1857. <http://teachingamericanhistory.org/library/document/speech-on-the-dred-scott-decision-2/>

[11] Stanton, Elizabeth Cady. "The Declaration of Sentiments." 1848. Seneca Falls Conference. *A History of Woman Suffrage* , vol. 1., p.70-71. Rochester, N.Y.: Fowler and Wells, 1889. <https://sourcebooks.fordham.edu/mod/senecafalls.asp>

Chapter Two

[12] "Thomas Hobbes (1588-1679)." BBC. 2014. <http://www.bbc.co.uk/history/historic_figures/hobbes_thomas.shtml>

[13] Page 10 reference: "A COMMONWEALTH is said to be instituted when a multitude of men do agree, and covenant, every one with every one, that to whatsoever man, or assembly of men, shall be given by the major part the right to present the person of them all, that is to say, to be their representative; every one, as well he that voted for it as he that voted against it, shall authorize all the actions and judgements of that man, or assembly of men, in the same manner as if they were his own, to the end to live peaceably amongst themselves, and be protected against other men. From this institution of a Commonwealth are derived all the rights and faculties of him, or them, on whom the sovereign power is conferred by the consent of the people assembled. [...] This great

authority being indivisible, and inseparably annexed to the sovereignty, there is little ground for the opinion of them that say of sovereign kings, though they be singulis majores, of greater power than every one of their subjects, yet they be universis minores, of less power than them all together. For if by all together, they mean not the collective body as one person, then all together and every one signify the same; and the speech is absurd. But if by all together, they understand them as one person (which person the sovereign bears), then the power of all together is the same with the sovereign's power; and so again the speech is absurd: which absurdity they see well enough when the sovereignty is in an assembly of the people; but in a monarch they see it not; and yet the power of sovereignty is the same in whomsoever it be placed. And as the power, so also the honour of the sovereign, ought to be greater than that of any or all the subjects. For in the sovereignty is the fountain of honour." ~ Thomas Hobbes, Leviathan

[14] Hobbes, Thomas. "Leviathan." 1651. Cited in the US Constitution Coach Kit. Franklin, TN: PowerThink Publishing, 2009. Electronic.

[15] Locke, John. "Second Treatise of Government." 1689. Cited in the US Constitution Coach Kit. Franklin, TN: PowerThink Publishing, 2009. Electronic.

[16] Otis, James. The Collected Political Writings of James Otis. Edited and with an Introduction by Richard Samuelson (Indianapolis: Liberty Fund, 2015). <http://oll.libertyfund.org/titles/2703>

[17] "The Magna Carta." 1215. Cited in the US Constitution Coach Kit. Franklin, TN: PowerThink Publishing, 2009. Electronic.

[18] Nelson, Jessica. "Magna Carta and counselling the King." The National Archives (UK). 15 June 2015.

<https://history.blog.gov.uk/2015/06/15/magna-carta-and-counselling-the-king/>

[19] Ohlmeyer, Jane H. "English Civil Wars." Encyclopedia Britannica. 17 August 2018. <https://www.britannica.com/event/English-Civil-Wars>

[20] "Why did people go to war in 1642? Case Study 1: 1637-39." The National Archives (UK). <http://www.nationalarchives.gov.uk/education/civilwar/g3/cs1/s2/#>

[21] "The English Bill of Rights." 1689. The Avalon Project. Yale Law School. <http://avalon.law.yale.edu/17th_century/england.asp>

[22] Jefferson, Thomas. "Declaration of Independence." 1776. Cited in the US Constitution Coach Kit. Franklin, TN: PowerThink Publishing, 2009. Electronic.

[23] Page 14 reference: "In one respect, the establishment of a common measure for representation and taxation will have a very salutary effect. As the accuracy of the census to be obtained by the Congress will necessarily depend, in a considerable degree, on the disposition, if not on the co-operation of the States, it is of great importance that the States should feel as little bias as possible to swell or to reduce the amount of their numbers. Were their share of representation alone to be governed by this rule, they would have an interest in exaggerating their inhabitants. Were the rule to decide their share of taxation alone, a contrary temptation would prevail. By extending the rule to both objects, the States will have opposite interests which will control and balance each other and produce the requisite impartiality." ~ James Madison, Federalist Paper 54

[24] Hamilton, Alexander. "Federalist Paper 35." 1788. Cited in the US Constitution Coach Kit. Franklin, TN: PowerThink Publishing, 2009. Electronic.

[25] Madison, James. "Federalist Paper 54." 1788. Cited in the US Constitution Coach Kit. Franklin, TN: PowerThink Publishing, 2009. Electronic.

[26] Crews, Ed. "Voting in Early America." 2007. Colonial Williamsburg Journal.
<http://www.history.org/foundation/journal/spring07/elections.cfm>

[27] "History of Voting in America." Washington – Secretary of State.
<https://www.sos.wa.gov/_assets/elections/history-of-voting-in-america-timeline.pdf>

Chapter Three

[28] Paine, Thomas. "Common Sense: The Call to Independence." 1776. Barron's Educational Series, Inc. 1975.

[29] Adams, Samuel. "Boston Gazette, 14 March 1768." First Amendment Watch. 2017.
<https://firstamendmentwatch.org/history-speaks-essays-samuel-adams-populus/>

[30] Feldman, Stephan M. "Free Expression and Democracy in America: A History." ReadHowYouWant.com. p. 87-89. 2010.
<https://books.google.com/books?id=lsNyBSw4p2AC&lpg=PA88&ots=vRNnZHrLzL&dq=there%20is%20nothing%20so%20fretting%20and%20vexatious&pg=PA88#v=onepage&q=there%20is%20nothing%20so%20fretting%20and%20vexatious&f=false>

[31] Solomon, Stephen D. "The Cost of Criticism." 2017. Colonial Williamsburg Journal. <http://www.history.org/Foundation/magazine/Winter17/PastForward.cfm>

[32] Mathewson, Joe. "State Guarantees of Freedom of the Press." 2006. MSU. <https://list.msu.edu/cgi-bin/wa?A3=ind0610d&L=AEJMC&E=0&P=2129165&B=--&T=text%2Fplain;%20charset=us-ascii>

[33] Milton, John. "Areopagitica." 1644. The John Milton Reading Room. Dartmouth. <https://www.dartmouth.edu/~milton/reading_room/areopagitica/text.html>

[34] Milton, John. "Areopagitica." 1644. Ed. Sid Parkinson. St. Lawrence Institute for the Advancement of Learning. Montreal, Quebec. <http://www.stlawrenceinstitute.org/vol14mit.html>

[35] "The English Bill of Rights." 1689. The Avalon Project. Yale Law School. <http://avalon.law.yale.edu/17th_century/england.asp>

[36] Beck, James M. "The Vanishing Rights of the States." P. 29-41. New York: George H. Doran Company. 1926.

[37] Lynch, Jack. "Wilkes, Liberty, and Number 45." 2003. Colonial Williamsburg Journal. <http://www.history.org/foundation/journal/summer03/wilkes.cfm>

[38] Wilkes, John. "The North Briton No. 45." 1763. The Constitution Society. <http://constitution.org/cmt/wilkes/north_briton_45.html>

[39] Beck, James M. "The Vanishing Rights of the States." P. 29-41. New York: George H. Doran Company. 1926.

[40] Bradley, Justice Joseph P. "Lead Opinion: Boyd v. United States 1886." U.S. Supreme Court. United States Reports: Cases Adjudged in the Supreme Court. Washington, D.C.: U.S. Government Printing Office, 1754–1997. Selections. Cited in the US Constitution Coach Kit. Franklin, TN: PowerThink Publishing, 2009. Electronic.

[41] Worden, Blair. "The English Civil Wars 1640-1660." P. 27-28, 90-91. London: Phoenix. 2009.

[42] Wohlers, Charles. "The Book of Common Prayer – 1549." Anglican.org. <http://justus.anglican.org/resources/bcp/1549/BCP_1549.htm>

[43] Worden, Blair. "The English Civil Wars 1640-1660." P. 96. London: Phoenix. 2009.

[44] Walther, Daniel. "Religious Motivations of the 'Mayflower' Pilgrims." 1957. Ministry Magazine. <https://www.ministrymagazine.org/archive/1957/08/religious-motivation-of-the-mayflower-pilgrims>

[45] Brooks, Rebecca Beatrice. "The History of Plymouth Colony." 2016. History of Massachusetts Blog. <http://historyofmassachusetts.org/plymouth-colony-history/>

[46] Brooks, Rebecca Beatrice. "The Great Puritan Migration." 2017. History of Massachusetts Blog. <http://historyofmassachusetts.org/the-great-puritan-migration/>

[47] "The Great Migration of Picky Puritans 1620-40." 2018. New England Historical Society. <http://www.newenglandhistoricalsociety.com/the-great-

migration-of-picky-puritans-1620-40/>

[48] Adams, Samuel. "The Rights of the Colonists." 1772. The Constitution Society.
<https://www.constitution.org/bcp/right_col.htm>

Chapter Four

[49] Bradley, Justice Joseph P. "Lead Opinion: Boyd v. United States 1886." U.S. Supreme Court. United States Reports: Cases Adjudged in the Supreme Court. Washington, D.C.: U.S. Government Printing Office, 1754–1997. Selections. Cited in the US Constitution Coach Kit. Franklin, TN: PowerThink Publishing, 2009. Electronic.

[50] Ibid.

[51] "Magna Carta." The British Library. 2018.
<https://www.bl.uk/magna-carta>

[52] Davis, GRC. "English Translation of Magna Carta." 2014. The British Library. Magna Carta (London: British Museum, 1963), pp. 23–33. <https://www.bl.uk/magna-carta/articles/magna-carta-english-translation>

[53] "Habeas Corpus Act: 1679." The British Library.
<http://www.bl.uk/learning/timeline/item104236.html>

[54] "Bill of Rights: British History." Encyclopedia Britannica.
<https://www.britannica.com/topic/Bill-of-Rights-British-history>

[55] "The English Bill of Rights." 1689. The Avalon Project. Yale Law School. <http://avalon.law.yale.edu/17th_century/england.asp>

[56] "The Colonial Crisis: 1750-1775." Lumen Learning. <https://courses.lumenlearning.com/boundless-ushistory/chapter/the-acts-of-parliament/>

[57] "1764 – Sugar Act." Stamp Act History.com. <http://www.stamp-act-history.com/sugar-act/1764-april-5-sugar-act/>

[58] "For Transporting Us Beyond The Seas To Be Tried For Pretended Offenses." Founding.com. The Claremont Institute. <http://founding.com/for-transporting-us-beyond-the-seas-to-be-tried-for-pretended-offenses/>

[59] Jefferson, Thomas. "Declaration of Independence." 1776. Cited in the US Constitution Coach Kit. Franklin, TN: PowerThink Publishing, 2009. Electronic.

[60] "The Constitution of the United States of America." Cited in the US Constitution Coach Kit. Franklin, TN: PowerThink Publishing, 2009. Electronic.

[61] Ibid. Article 1, Sect 9.

[62] Ibid. Article 3, Sect. 2.

[63] Ibid. Article 3, Sect. 3.

Chapter Five

[64] Locke, John. "Second Treatise of Government." 1689. Cited in the US Constitution Coach Kit. Franklin, TN: PowerThink Publishing, 2009. Electronic.

[65] "Lexington and Concord: The Shot Heard 'Round the World." American Battlefield Trust.

<https://www.battlefields.org/learn/articles/lexington-and-concord-shot-heard-round-world>

[66] "Battles of Lexington and Concord." Encyclopedia Britannica. <https://www.britannica.com/event/Battles-of-Lexington-and-Concord>

[67] Fischer, David Hackett. "Paul Revere's Ride." P. 43. New York: Oxford Unity Press. 1994.

[68] "When Paul Revere Road to New Hampshire." 2017. New England Historical Society. <http://www.newenglandhistoricalsociety.com/paul-revere-rode-new-hampshire/>

[69] "Powder Alarm (Cambridge Massachusetts)." Encyclopedia of the American Revolution: Library of Military History. Encyclopedia.com. 2018. <https://www.encyclopedia.com/history/encyclopedias-almanacs-transcripts-and-maps/powder-alarm-cambridge-massachusetts>

[70] "John Rowe Diary 11, 1-4 September 1774, Pages 1901-1902." The Massachusetts Historical Society. <http://www.masshist.org/revolution/doc-viewer.php?item_id=533&mode=nav&old=1>

[71] Fischer, David Hackett. "Paul Revere's Ride." P. 51. New York: Oxford Unity Press. 1994.

[72] Ibid. P. 53-57.

[73] "When Paul Revere Road to New Hampshire." 2017. New England Historical Society. <http://www.newenglandhistoricalsociety.com/paul-revere-rode-new-hampshire/>

[74] Fischer, David Hackett. "Paul Revere's Ride." P. 58-64. New York: Oxford Unity Press. 1994.

[75] Harris, Gordon. "Leslie's Retreat: Or, How the Revolutionary War almost began in Salem: February 26, 1775." 2014. Historic Ipswich. <https://historicipswich.org/2014/07/05/leslies-retreat-or-how-the-revolutionary-war-almost-began-in-salem/>

[76] Seger, Donna. "Resistance and Retreat in Salem, 1775." 2014. Streets of Salem. <https://streetsofsalem.com/2014/02/26/resistance-and-retreat-in-salem-1775/>

[77] Warren, Joseph. "The Suffolk Resolves." 1774. <https://www.nps.gov/mima/learn/education/upload/the%20suffolk%20resolves.pdf>

[78] "The Suffolk Resolves." Encyclopedia Britannica. <https://www.britannica.com/event/Suffolk-Resolves>

[79] "Fyrd." Encyclopedia Britannica. <https://www.britannica.com/topic/fyrd>

[80] "Assize of Arms." 1181. <http://www.constitution.org/eng/assizarm.htm>

[81] "An Overview: Assize of Arms." Oxford Reference. <http://www.oxfordreference.com/view/10.1093/oi/authority.20110803095424186>

[82] "Edward III Bans Football, Promotes Archery." History Channel. <https://www.historychannel.com.au/articles/edward-iii-bans-football-promotes-archery/>

[83] Turner, Nicola. "Old Archery Games." 2015. Bow International.
<http://www.bow-international.com/features/traditional/old-archery-games/>

[84] "The English Bill of Rights." 1689. The Avalon Project. Yale Law School. <http://avalon.law.yale.edu/17th_century/england.asp>

[85] Fischer, David Hackett. "Paul Revere's Ride." P. 151-162. New York: Oxford Unity Press. 1994.

[86] "Madison's Introduction to the Bill of Rights." 1789. USConstitution.net. <https://www.usconstitution.net/madisonbor.html>

Chapter Six

[87] Page 35 reference: "No position appears to me more true than this; that the General Government cannot effectually exist without reserving to the States the possession of their local rights. They are the instruments upon which the Union must frequently depend for the support and execution of their powers, however immediately operating upon the people, and not upon the States." ~ Mr. Pinckney, Journal of the Federalist Convention Monday, June 25th, 1787

[88] Madison, James. "Journal of the Federal Convention." 2 vols. Chicago: Albert, Scott & Co, 1893, originally published in 1840. Reprint. E.H. Scott. Cited in the US Constitution Coach Kit. Franklin, TN: PowerThink Publishing, 2009. Electronic.

[89] Schweikart, Larry, and Michael Allen. "A Patriot's History of the United States." P. 116-119. New York: Penguin Group. 2004.

[90] Lloyd, Gordon. "Introduction to the Antifederalists." TeachingAmericanHistory.org. <http://teachingamericanhistory.org/fed-antifed/antifederalist/>

[91] Madison, James. "Journal of the Federal Convention." 2 vols. Chicago: Albert, Scott & Co, 1893, originally published in 1840. Reprint. E.H. Scott. Cited in the US Constitution Coach Kit. Franklin, TN: PowerThink Publishing, 2009. Electronic.

[92] Page 39 reference: "The powers delegated by the proposed Constitution to the federal government are few and defined. Those which are to remain in the State governments are numerous and indefinite. The former will be exercised on external objects, as war, peace, negotiation, and foreign commerce; with which last the power of taxation will, for the most part, be connected. The powers reserved to the several States will extend to all the objects which, in the ordinary course of affairs, concern the lives, liberties, and properties of the people, and the internal order, improvement, and prosperity of the State." ~ James Madison, Federalist Paper #45

[93] "The Constitution of the United States of America." Cited in the US Constitution Coach Kit. Franklin, TN: PowerThink Publishing, 2009. Electronic.

[94] Madison, James. "Federalist Paper 45." 1788. Cited in the US Constitution Coach Kit. Franklin, TN: PowerThink Publishing, 2009. Electronic.

[95] "The Constitution of the United States of America." Cited in the US Constitution Coach Kit. Franklin, TN: PowerThink Publishing, 2009. Electronic.

[96] "Madison's Introduction to the Bill of Rights." 1789. USConstitution.net. <https://www.usconstitution.net/madisonbor.html>

Chapter Seven

[97] Johnson, Donald B. "The Progressive Party Platform of 1912." National Party Platforms, 1840–1976. Supplement 1980. Champaign-Urbana: University of Illinois Press, 1982. Cited in the US Constitution Coach Kit. Franklin, TN: PowerThink Publishing, 2009. Electronic, ed

[98] Slack, Megan. "From the Archives: President Teddy Roosevelt's New Nationalism Speech." 1910. Obama White House Archives. 2011. <https://obamawhitehouse.archives.gov/blog/2011/12/06/archive s-president-teddy-roosevelts-new-nationalism-speech>

[99] "The Constitution of the United States of America." Cited in the US Constitution Coach Kit. Franklin, TN: PowerThink Publishing, 2009. Electronic.

[100] Ibid.

[101] Page 46 reference: "The Progressive party, believing that a free people should have the power from time to time to amend their fundamental law so as to adapt it progressively to the changing needs of the people, pledges itself to provide a more easy and expeditious method of amending the Federal Constitution." ~ The Progressive Party Platform of 1912

[102] Johnson, Donald B. "The Progressive Party Platform of 1912." National Party Platforms, 1840–1976. Supplement 1980. Champaign-Urbana: University of Illinois Press, 1982. Cited in the US Constitution Coach Kit. Franklin, TN: PowerThink Publishing, 2009. Electronic, ed

[103] "The Constitution of the United States of America." Cited in the US Constitution Coach Kit. Franklin, TN: PowerThink Publishing, 2009. Electronic.

[104] Garner, Anne. "'FEAR Narcotic Drugs!' The Passage of the Harrison Act." The New York Academy of Medicine. 2014. <https://nyamcenterforhistory.org/2014/12/17/fear-narcotic-drugs-the-passage-of-the-harrison-act/>

[105] "Did You Know... Marijuana Was Once a Legal Cross-Border Import?." U.S. Customs and Border Protection. 2015. <https://www.cbp.gov/about/history/did-you-know/marijuana>

Chapter Eight

[106] Doherty, Carroll. "Key takeaways on Americans' growing partisan divide over political values." 2017. Pew Research Center. < http://www.pewresearch.org/fact-tank/2017/10/05/takeaways-on-americans-growing-partisan-divide-over-political-values/>

[107] Sasse, Ben. "Sasse on Kavanaugh Hearing: 'We Can And We Should Do Better Than This.'" 2018. U.S. Senator for Nebraska. <https://www.sasse.senate.gov/public/index.cfm/2018/9/sasse-on-kavanaugh-hearing-we-can-and-we-should-do-better-than-this>

[108] Eilperin, Juliet and Damien Paletta. "Trump administration cancels hundreds of Obama-era regulations." 2017. Washington Post. <https://www.washingtonpost.com/business/economy/trump-administration-cancels-hundreds-of-obama-era-regulations/2017/07/20/55f501cc-6d68-11e7-96ab-5f38140b38cc_story.html?utm_term=.bdfd99cf3717>

[109] Reynolds, Glenn Harlan. "Reynolds: You are probably breaking the law right now." 2015. USA Today. <https://www.usatoday.com/story/opinion/2015/03/29/crime-law-criminal-unfair-column/70630978/>

[110] Page 52 reference: "The President is to be the commander-in-chief of the army and navy of the United States. In this respect his authority would be nominally the same with that of the king of Great Britain, but in substance much inferior to it. It would amount to nothing more than the supreme command and direction of the military and naval forces, as first general and admiral of the Confederacy; while that of the British king extends to the declaring of war and to the raising and regulating of fleets and armies—all which, by the Constitution under consideration, would appertain to the legislature." ~ Alexander Hamilton, Federalist Paper #69

[111] Washington, George. "From George Washington To William Moultrie, 23 August 1793." 1793. National Archives. <https://founders.archives.gov/documents/Washington/05-13-02-0381>

[112] Madison, James. "James Madison to Thomas Jefferson." 1798. <http://press-pubs.uchicago.edu/founders/documents/a1_8_11s8.html>

[113] Jefferson, Thomas. "From Thomas Jefferson To United States Congress, 6 December 1805." 1805. National Archives. <https://founders.archives.gov/documents/Jefferson/99-01-02-2779>

[114] Hamilton, Alexander. "Federalist Paper 69." 1788. Cited in the US Constitution Coach Kit. Franklin, TN: PowerThink Publishing, 2009. Electronic.

[115] Woods, Thomas. "The Constitution is Clear on Presidential War Powers." 2009. Tenth Amendment Center. <https://tenthamendmentcenter.com/2009/12/30/the-constitution-is-clear-on-presidential-war-powers/>

[116] Ackerman, Spencer. " 'A Constitutional Crisis:' the CIA turns on the Senate." 2016. The Guardian. <https://www.theguardian.com/us-news/2016/sep/10/cia-senate-investigation-constitutional-crisis-daniel-jones>

[117] Ackerman, Spencer. "CIA admits to spying on Senate staffers." 2014. The Guardian. <https://www.theguardian.com/world/2014/jul/31/cia-admits-spying-senate-staffers>

[118] Attkisson, Sharyl. "CIA's 'surveillance state' is operating against us all." 2018. The Hill. <https://thehill.com/opinion/national-security/414804-surveillance-state-is-alive-well-and-operating-against-us-all>

[119] Siddiqui, Sabrina. "Senators OK With Spying On Citizens, But Outraged It Happened To Congress." 2014. HuffPost. <https://www.huffingtonpost.com/2014/03/11/cia-spying-congress_n_4945584.html>

[120] Liptak, Kevin. "Rand Paul: James Clapper was Lying." 2013. CNN. <http://politicalticker.blogs.cnn.com/2013/06/18/rand-paul-james-clapper-was-lying/>

[121] MacAskill, Ewen and Gabriel Dance. "NSA FILES." 2013. The Guardian. <https://www.theguardian.com/world/interactive/2013/nov/01/snowden-nsa-files-surveillance-revelations-decoded#section/1>

[122] Hattem, Julian. "Spy head: I didn't lie to Congress." 2016. The Hill. <https://thehill.com/policy/national-security/269751-spy-head-i-didnt-lie-to-congress>

[123] MacAskill, Ewen. "Edward Snowden: What would happen if he went home – pardon or prison?" 2015. The Guardian. <https://www.theguardian.com/us-news/2015/mar/04/edward-snowden-what-would-happen-if-he-went-home-pardon-or-prison>

[124] Shiffman, John and Kristina Cooke. "Exclusive: U.S. directs agents to cover up program used to investigate Americans." 2013. Reuters. <https://www.reuters.com/article/us-dea-sod-idUSBRE97409R20130805>

[125] Apuzzo, Matt. "'I Small Cash': How the A.T.F. Spent Millions Unchecked." 2017. New York Times. <https://www.nytimes.com/2017/09/08/us/atf-tobacco-cigarettes.html>

[126] Attkisson, Sheryl. "Documents: ATF used 'Fast and Furious' to make the case for gun regulations." 2011. CBS News. <https://www.cbsnews.com/news/documents-atf-used-fast-and-furious-to-make-the-case-for-gun-regulations/>

Made in the USA
Monee, IL
03 November 2020